WEIRD AND WONDERFUL
AUTOS

Published 1975 by Enterprise Books
Secausus, New Jersey

Copyright © 1975 by Intercontinental Book Productions
Library of Congress Catalog Card Number 74–24827

ISBN 0–89009–030–0

Printed and bound in Belgium

WEIRD AND WONDERFUL
AUTOS

By Mike Hill

ENTERPRISE BOOKS

Contents

Introduction

In most parts of the world the motor car is so much part of life that it's hard to imagine a time when the horseless carriage was considered a total novelty. It's worth remembering too that even today there are parts of the world into which the self-powered machine has yet to penetrate, where even the most ordinary family car would be considered weird and wonderful.

However, accepting the social and economic importance of the motor car today, we can look back over its history during this century and find machines which even now are considered distinctly oddball.

Some cars are odd because their builders have tried to be different, because they have tried a new solution to the problem of providing a self-propelled carriage. Or because they have excelled in some way — for example, the quickest, the largest, the most powerful, and 'firsts' in various fields.

Today, with much emphasis on technical development, there is a movement dedicated to creating something individual from the clinical mass-produced car — the customizers, hot-rodders and the various associated 'street freaks.'

They are all here in the weird and wonderful world of the motor car — the oddities of yesteryear, the nutty creations of today, the record breakers, the show cars, the dragsters, the hot-rods, from wilder to wildest, from 0–622 mph.

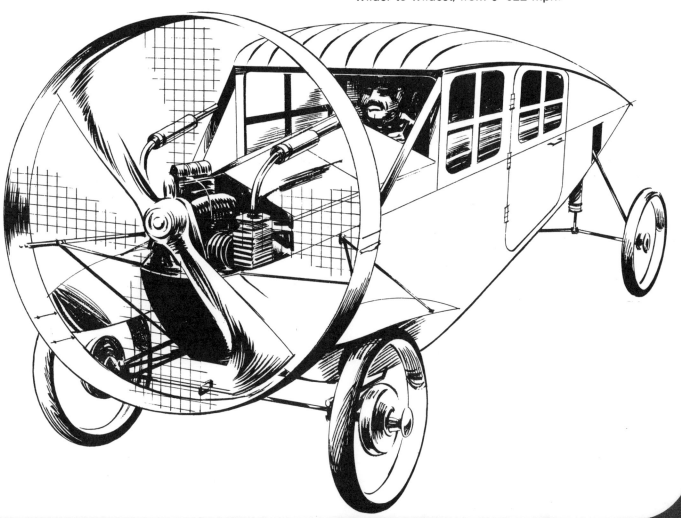

Odd Ones Out

Octo-Auto

Reeves' Octo-Auto was made in America in 1911 and looked like a normal car with an additional axle back and front. No less than three pairs of wheels did the steering – the inventor claimed it reduced tire wear!

It's easy to look back at any period in motoring history and believe that every car made was in some way weird and wonderful. Imagine too the Victorian motorist trying to make sense of some of our 1970s sophistry in engineering – the front wheel-drive Mini, capable of 90 mph from 1,000 cc, would seem as odd to him as the early attempts at a horseless carriage seem to us today.

Sunbeam Mabley

Cars have been made with many permutations of wheels, but this 1901 Sunbeam Mabley has one of the oddest of the four-wheel arrangements with a single wheel front and rear and a pair in the center. Passengers sat facing sideways. It had a single 326-cc engine driving the central axle, and tiller steering.

But certainly the early days of motoring were the real pioneering days, with new ideas being tried all the time, many mistakes made, and a good many real freaks designed and created in the name of automobile engineering.

Today, with mass production, most of the weird and wonderfuls are purpose built either to be just plain different or for a special purpose – show, racing, record breaking, movies etc.

Some cars stood out from others because of the ingenuity of their engineering. The 1897 Leon Bollée, for example, was a lightweight three-wheeler with a seat for the intrepid passenger perched low in front. Bollée designed a horizontal engine which drove the rear wheels through a patented chain speed lever; this released the belt drive from the engine and shifted gear at the same time. Pressing the lever forward tightened the belt in the new gear speed.

Lanchester too is a name much renowned for the original thinking which went into its engineering – in fact, many of the ideas pioneered on Lanchesters would still be sophisticated on today's cars. The 1901 model was noted for its mechanical smoothness – its worm drive cut out the need for chains or belts – the patented new method of igniting the petrol air mix, and its automatic lubrication.

But over the years, even during times of rapid development in the auto industry, there have been some real freaks.

With today's emphasis on electric power for city use, it's interesting to note that in 1899 Frenchman Camille Jenatzy became a world record breaker with an electric-powered device called *Jamais Contente* (never satisfied). Apart from its unorthodox power, it's also notable as one of the earliest attempts at car streamlining – its torpedo-like body enabled Jenatzy to reach nearly 66 mph, which was considered suicidal at a time when drivers in the UK had been used to following a man with a red flag!

Cars have been designed with almost any number of wheels. No one has actually made a mono-wheel, but there has been at least one two-wheeler. The English Wolseley company tried one once, as did an American gentleman named J. S. Booth. He was later to become known for a more successful small car, but in 1913 he introduced his Bi-Autogo. It had a pair of small auxiliary wheels, but apparently these were lowered only for parking purposes; the theory was that they retracted as speed built up, so that the vehicle kept upright under its own momentum, motorbike fashion. Apart from its bizarre layout, the Bi-Autogo was also interesting in that it pioneered the V8 engine in America.

From two wheels to eight and another American invention – the Octo-Auto, designed by M. O. Reeves in 1911, which appears to have been a perfectly well-balanced four-seat touring car with an additional axle back and front. Reeves' theory was that tire wear was *reduced* by spreading the load! The axle under the back seat was driven by the engine. The three remaining axles all steered — which would seem like engineering for its own sake. It wasn't a success, but the principle survived; multi-steering axles are used today on some commercial trucks.

Car designers sprang from all manner of sources, and some of the oddest creations came from the aircraft industry at a time when that industry was even less developed than its earthbound counterpart.

Curiously, the 1921 Rumpler resembled a boat as much as a plane, although its German designer, Edmund Rumpler, was an aeronautics engineer. Despite its weird looks, it was efficient in 'windcheating,' and even today the underside of a modern car is not as aerodynamically efficient as the smooth-hulled Rumpler. The driver sat, pilot fashion, on his own at the front of the tear-drop shaped body with the passengers in the center. The engine was rear-mounted and also followed aircraft practice, having six cylinders in W-formation. The Rumpler was no lightweight, but the Siemens 36-hp engine made good use of the aerodynamics to achieve 70 mph. In 2·6

Leon Bollée's tandem chair

Leon Bollée's famous tandem chair with rear-mounted 650-cc engine. Speed of the engine was controlled by governing the exhaust valve opening on the single-cylinder engine.

litre form, with Rumpler's own engine, 80 mph was possible, the gearbox coupled directly to the rear axle for maximum efficiency.

Even more like an aircraft was the French Leyat of 1923, which looked as if it needed only a pair of wings to launch itself over the Eiffel Tower. Marcel Leyat actually had models in production for a while and both closed and open bodies were available. The air-cooled 1200-cc twin engine drove directly to a huge propeller up front; this was encircled by a wooden rim and wire mesh, presumably to keep the good French people from falling into the works and turning themselves into *pâté*! There were no gears and the

Atlantic

The Atlantic had an air-cooled two-cylinder engine and was made in Germany.

Looking more like a film stunt car than a military vehicle, the De Lesseps was built for the French army's winter manoeuvres — hence the skis and the propeller at the rear for snow propulsion. It was powered by a straight-eight aero engine.

Is it a plane, a boat, a train? Edmund Rumpler worked extensively in the aircraft industry before turning his hand to cars in the 1920s. This tear-drop streamliner was built in 1921 and had a rear-mounted six-cylinder engine in W-formation which was built in one unit with the gearbox and final drive.

Crossley built this six-wheeler cross-country car for King George V with drive through the rear four wheels. It was shown at the London Motor Show in 1930 but did not go into production.

steering was on the rear wheels. It must have been lethal to drive, too, since the brakes, on the front wheels only were controlled by separate pedals, one for each wheel. The standard machine, due to its light weight, was said to achieve 50 mph, although one driver (pilot?) apparently managed twice that on a race track.

Social and economic conditions bred oddities, usually short-lived, often still-born. The immediate post-Second World War years in Europe meant a big industrial reorganisation, and Emile Mathis found himself once more back in the French bit of Alsace. Mathis had been one of Europe's top four producers in the 1920s and '30s but had lost impetus before the Second World War.

In 1946, Mathis returned from America with an idea for an economy car for the masses. He called it the 333 — three seats, three wheels, and using ·66 gals. of gasoline for every 62 miles covered. The unitary bodywork had the look of a frightened easter egg with a front not unlike the later VW coupé that Karmann Ghia produced. On the face

Rumpler

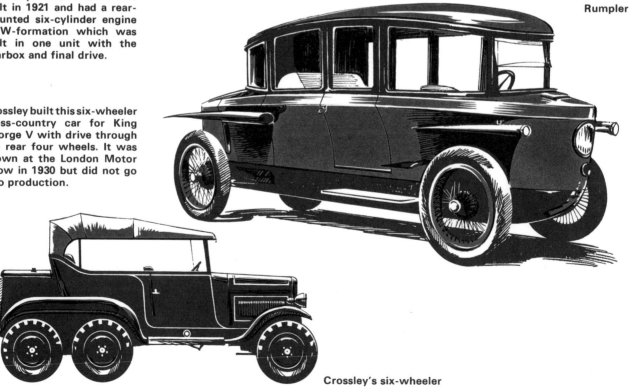

Crossley's six-wheeler

8

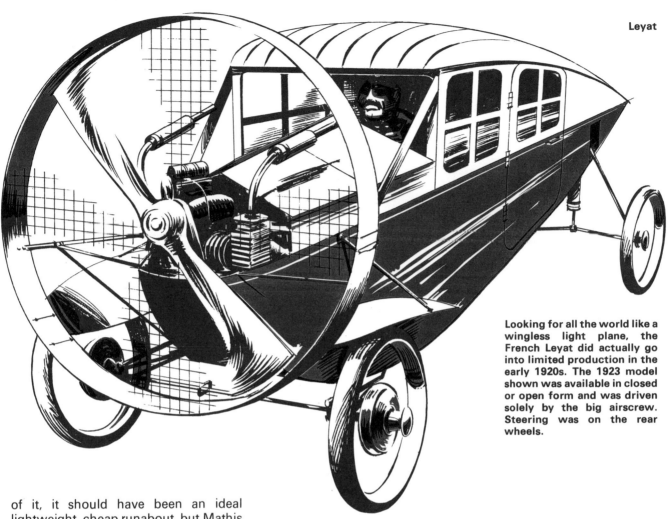

Looking for all the world like a wingless light plane, the French Leyat did actually go into limited production in the early 1920s. The 1923 model shown was available in closed or open form and was driven solely by the big airscrew. Steering was on the rear wheels.

of it, it should have been an ideal lightweight, cheap runabout, but Mathis was refused permission to start production — industry was still very much state controlled while the country got back on its feet. For its day it had several innovations — hydraulically-boosted front brakes, four-speed synchromesh gearbox, and coil and wishbone independent front suspension. It was light enough to manage 68 mph and 80 mpg from its 700-cc engine.

Aurora safety sedan

Stylists' nightmare — the 1958 Aurora safety sedan, designed by an American priest, looked as if it were being driven in reverse. It was offered with Cadillac or Lincoln engines.

Emile Mathis, one of the big four car makers in Europe before the Second World War, returned to France in 1945 with a new idea — a three-seater, three-wheeler economy car for the people. It made a lot of sense for the post-war economy, but Mathis was prevented by government restrictions from putting it into production.

Mathis's 333

9

Early Greats

Marcus, 1875

Siegfried Marcus was a brilliant engineer who gave his attention to every sort of invention, from dentistry aids to motor cars. Seen here is his second car, built in 1875, although he had completed a working vehicle as early as 1865.

The 'Curved Dash' Runabout, built in 1903 by the Oldsmobile company, was the world's first mass-production motor car. Several thousand were made between 1901 and 1905.

The early oddities on the previous page could well give the impression that motoring's pioneers were exceptionally bizarre. At the time, of course, every automobile engineer was looked upon to one degree or another as a crank. Doubtless there were cranks among them — but the majority of these early inventors were sane and sincere, if not always successful. However, amid the many whimsical creations there were some real gems — machines to be taken seriously . . . machines which represented real stepping stones in the development of automobile engineering.

Regarded by many as one of the first 'stepping stones' is the vehicle constructed by the Austrian Siegfried Marcus, which is reputed to be the first internal combustion engine carriage, built in 1875.

It was, indeed, one of the early greats, although it could have been a lot greater, had Marcus had the patience to persevere with his invention. Unfortunately, the man was too prolific an inventor to spend time perfecting anything. When the police forbade him to continue testing his automobile on the public highway on account of the noise which the vehicle produced, the inventor lost interest and turned his attention to another of his many brain-children.

Ten years later, engineer Karl Benz produced his first offering, a spidery-looking three-wheeled machine which was based on a lightweight frame and ran on slim, bicycle-type wheels. The front one of these was the 'steering' wheel. Why *three* wheels? No reason, really, other than that Benz found that this formula was workable. Remember that Benz was one of the very earliest pioneers and so had little data of any consequence on which he could base his ideas. In view of this, his achievement, which came to fruition in 1885, was a remarkable one. It notched up its place in history on two counts — as the first internal-combustion driven vehicle to go into production, and consequently as the first 'seed' of the industry which took root and gave life to the automobile world as we know it today.

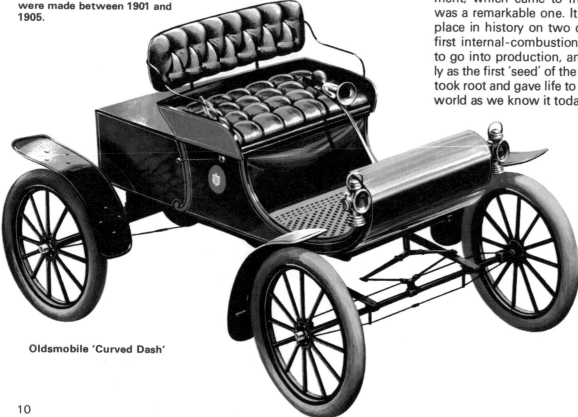

Oldsmobile 'Curved Dash'

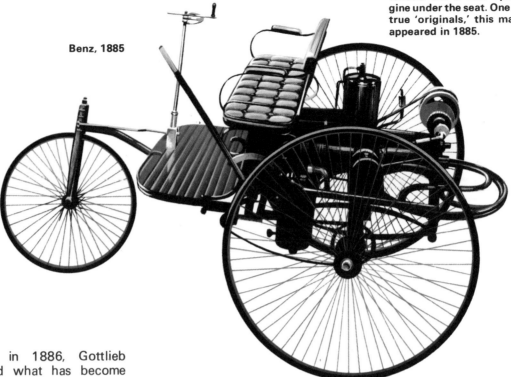

Benz, 1885

A year later, in 1886, Gottlieb Daimler produced what has become recognized as the first *four*-wheeled gasoline-driven machine. Unlike Benz, Daimler had concentrated on developing his engine; he was not, at that time, too concerned with the vehicle — only the means of propulsion. Hence his first car was a motorized horse-drawn carriage — minus the horses, of course!

America, as one would expect, takes her share of the honors for the early greats. To the famous Oldsmobile company goes the distinction of being the first to put a car into mass production.

The year was 1903, and the car was known as the 'Curved Dash' — a name earned by its running board, which was turned up at the front like a sled. It could achieve a top speed of 20 mph, was water-cooled and bore leaf-spring suspension, a principle which is still in use the world over.

Of course, a look at the early greats of motoring history, however brief, would not be complete without a mention of the one car which completely revolutionized the motor industry, a car which has become nothing less than a legend — the Ford Model T.

Known as 'The automobile that motorized America,' the Model T made its appearance in 1908 and quickly won a place in the hearts — and garages — of the footsore pedestrians of the American continent. What made the car so popular was the simplicity of its controls, its sound suspension, its classic good looks — and, of course, its useful top speed of around 45 mph.

In 1902, it is reported, Henry Ford announced, 'I will build a car for the great multitudes.' He was as good as his word. During the 19 years (from 1908 to 1927) that the Model T was in production, the public snapped up an incredible 15,007,033 of them!

In order to keep the experiments on his motor carriage secret, Gottlieb Daimler ostensibly purchased a horse-drawn carriage as a gift for his wife. He set about replacing the horses with a light gasoline engine — and in 1886 had the vehicle on the road, performing at 9 mph.

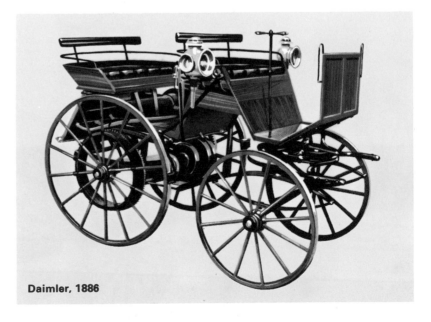

Daimler, 1886

Rocket Cars

Opel's Rak 1

Opel's Rak 1 at rest. With eight rockets in the tail, this ungainly machine achieved 65 mph in 8 seconds – an acceleration which few modern sports cars can boast !

The Wingfoot Express was built by Walt Arfons for an attempt at the Land Speed Record. Packed into its special delta shape was a battery of 25 J.A.T.O. (jet-assisted take-off) 1,000 lb thrust units. These fired in sequence – but failed to produce enough thrust to take the record. The Express's best speed was 580 mph.

Ever since the horseless carriage was invented, designers have sought and tried many different methods of propulsion. One of the most dramatic has been rocket power, which of course does away with the need for power-consuming transmission, relying solely on the force of the rocket jet to provide propulsion.

Rocketry has become very highly developed in the world's space programs, and although it is not likely to be a serious contender as a means of road transport, several weird and wonderful vehicles have been tried. It's a rocket-powered machine that currently holds the land speed record at well over 600 mph (pages 18–21).

That's a recent piece of technology, of course, but rocket power was first tried back in 1928 by the German Opel concern. They built three machines, named Rak 1, 2 and 3 (*rakete* being the

German for rocket). Rak 1 looked more like an Edwardian racer, high and ungainly. It was designed by Vallier and Sander, and with Kurt Volkhart at the wheel it reached 65 mph in only 8 seconds in April 1928. It was powered by eight rockets in the tail.

A month later Rak 2 appeared, a much more radical machine, low and cigar-shaped with a chopped-off tail in which 24 rockets were set. Apart from its rocketry, Rak 2 was interesting for its big aerofoils, which helped to keep the machine on the track. Aerofoils are now a vital part of modern racing car design. 2,000 spectators at the Avus circuit saw von Opel, son of the founder, achieve 125 mph in Rak 2 in May 1928.

The following month saw the appearance of Rak 3. Opel realized that there was little future in rocket-powered road machines, and Rak 3 was a bare chassis with a cab and a 22-rocket power-pack in the tail. It ran on a 5-mile stretch of railway track in June 1928 and, with the rockets igniting in stages, achieved a maximum speed of 160 mph. From here it was a short step to rocket flight – and a rocket plane flew in September of the same year with Fritz von Opel at the controls.

Apart from Gary Gabelich's record machine, one of the weirdest modern rocket machines is Jack McClure's go-kart which makes exhibition runs at drag strips in the United States. It looks

Wingfoot Express

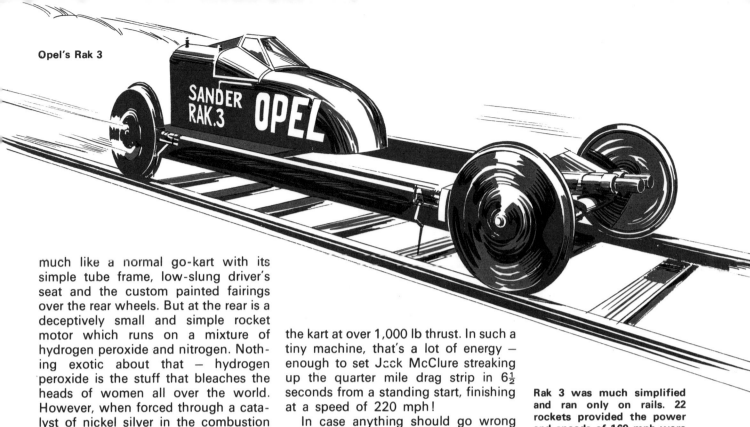

Opel's Rak 3

much like a normal go-kart with its simple tube frame, low-slung driver's seat and the custom painted fairings over the rear wheels. But at the rear is a deceptively small and simple rocket motor which runs on a mixture of hydrogen peroxide and nitrogen. Nothing exotic about that — hydrogen peroxide is the stuff that bleaches the heads of women all over the world. However, when forced through a catalyst of nickel silver in the combustion chamber, the temperature in the chamber reaches over 1,350°F and the mixture increases in volume 600 times over to produce steam which is then forced through a 2-inch nozzle at the rear of

the kart at over 1,000 lb thrust. In such a tiny machine, that's a lot of energy — enough to set Jack McClure streaking up the quarter mile drag strip in $6\frac{1}{2}$ seconds from a standing start, finishing at a speed of 220 mph!

In case anything should go wrong McClure has a special parachute built into his fireproof suit; this would jerk him out of his seat to a height of 50–100 feet before the 'chute opened to lower him to the ground.

Rak 3 was much simplified and ran only on rails. 22 rockets provided the power and speeds of 160 mph were achieved.

Rocket-powered go-kart

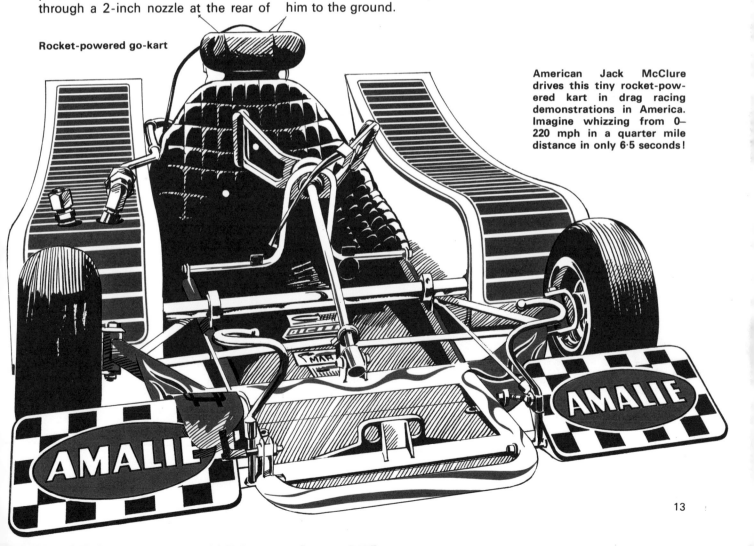

American Jack McClure drives this tiny rocket-powered kart in drag racing demonstrations in America. Imagine whizzing from 0–220 mph in a quarter mile distance in only 6·5 seconds!

Steam Cars

Bollée's steam omnibus of 1873 – one of the pioneers of the pivoted front wheel. Its 8,000 lb bulk was transported at 25 mph by its 20 hp engines.

Bollée's steam omnibus

The 1894 di Dion Bouton steam tractor, which, according to a journal of the time, 'draws a carriage like a horse, and develops (though with a powerful engine it must be admitted) a speed absolutely beyond comparison, especially uphill.' The machine achieved 11·6 mph!

Bouton's steam tractor

Generally credited as being the first horseless carriage, Cugnot's 1769 *fardier* had a massive boiler overhanging the front wheel which added considerably to the weight of the tiller steering. It moved at 2½ mph but had to stop every 15 minutes for water.

It's ironic that the steam-powered car, often dismissed as a thing of the past, may well turn out to be the car of the future. Steam has never achieved great success in a road machine, although it did contribute a great part to the mechanization of agriculture and in-

dustry. But there have been successful steamers – names like Stanley, Doble and White are legendary – and production steam cars were made right into the mid-1930s. Now, with the rising cost of oil and the realization that oil as a natural resource may one day be expended, more thought is again being given to steam power as a source of transport. The attractions are simplicity, and the relatively low level of contamination to the atmosphere.

Steam power requires a boiler and heat for that boiler to produce the steam which then operates a piston or pistons to produce motion. The drawback has been the length of time needed to raise the boiler to operating pressure. Early steam engines could take 20 minutes to get up steam, but with boiler development this was cut down to one minute by 1932 in the Doble steamer; using a Primus-type gasoline burner to boil water quickly for a head of steam. Today, 'flash' boilers – similar to those used in domestic heating boilers and hot water systems – can give almost instant heat and thus steam.

What is generally credited as being the first car, Cugnot's *fardier* cart, was steam-powered. It was built in 1769, and a year later Cugnot completed a more refined carriage version at his government's request. It had a huge boiler shaped like the bowl of a concrete

Cugnot's *fardier*

mixer; this was suspended forward of the single front wheel and a two-cylinder engine directly over the wheel. The whole arrangement had to turn with the wheel, which made steering with the tiller less than accurate, but at least it was truly a horseless carriage, able to move under its own power — even if it was at only 2½ mph! Little development was carried out on the machine since it had to stop every 15 minutes for water and pause for at least as long at every stop to allow the pressure to build up again.

Oddly, it was in America — the country which became most committed to the development of the internal combustion engine — that steam development continued. Stanley and White both developed cars for competition in the early part of this century, and in Edwardian times were still trading on the successes of their racers. In 1905 Stanley produced a low torpedo-like device called the Beetle; this passed 127 mph for the world land speed record in the hands of Fred Marriott, who in the following year became airborne in a similar car after he had exceeded 150 mph. But by 1911 the short-lived enthusiasm for steam cars had died away in both Europe and America. Several attempts were made in the 1920s to revive steam for passenger cars, most of which died

and its devotees claim that it could run on almost anything that would burn.

Today the development of the internal combustion engine has enabled car builders to make machines which are smooth, clean and economic — the properties which previously gave steam power an advantage over the internal combustion engine.

However, the realization that millions of gasoline-powered engines on our roads are not only polluting the atmosphere but are also using up the world's oil reserves at a frightening rate has led to renewed interest in steam. Most of the world's major car corporations have spent money in the last ten years on steam development, although none has put a steamer into production. Alec Issigonis, designer of the Mini, has made steam development his personal 'baby,' and Bill Lear, of Lear-Jet fame, has spent millions of dollars on steam research, resulting in a steam-powered bus engine which has proved its worth, even if it isn't yet in production. Increasingly stiff legislation all over the world may force the internal combustion engine makers to put more serious research into steam in the future, and it has been suggested that a steamer, with nuclear power providing the heat source for the steam, may be our transport for the future.

Goldsworthy Gurney's steam carriage

Goldsworthy Gurney's steam carriage — a sort of stage coach minus horses — was built in the late 1920s and could carry 21 passengers. It recorded an average speed of 15 mph.

almost as soon as they were born, with one exception — Doble, another American make which survived from 1924 to 1932. Doble developed the engineering side of the steam carriage to such a degree that it priced itself out of existence. What had set out to be simple, reliable transport became far from simple to build and a Doble of the early 1930s cost more than twice as much as a Rolls Royce. But it did prove the value of steam against the internal combustion engine of the time; it was smooth, effortless power, clean and quick to heat,

Stanley steam car

Road-going steam cars in Edwardian times looked little different from their internal combustion counterparts. This was a Stanley of 1911 which had two horizontal cylinders producing 10 hp between them. Sadly, most steam car makers died out before the First World War.

The Giants

The original Chitty Chitty Bang Bang – the name came from the sound of the 23-litre aero engine. Chittys 2 and 3 were built mainly for touring and had smaller aero engines.

The 'original' Chitty Chitty Bang Bang

19-foot-long sculpted fiberglass body hides a 26-litre Rolls Royce Merlin engine from a Second World War Spitfire. Capable of 200 mph, this Rolls custom car is used daily on the roads of England.

Rolls Royce 'special'

Big and beautiful, Type 41 Royale was Ettore Bugatti's crowning glory – at $250,000 for the chassis alone it was for crown heads only!

The quest for power, either for racing or for a bigger, better, faster road car, has led to the construction of many interesting freaks. As you'll see in the next chapter, many giant cars were built for record breaking, using the biggest, most powerful engines available – often aircraft engines. But other giants were built for track racing at speed circuits like Brooklands, and others for the road.

The film *Chitty Chitty Bang Bang* took its name from one of the most notorious giants of all. The original Chitty – or Chittys, for there were three in all – were built for wealthy racer

Count Louis Zborowski in the early 1920s. The Count loved fast cars and racing and wanted the biggest, fastest machine that would be suitable for both road and track.

Chitty 1 was a monster, built in the Count's own workshops on a lengthened and strengthened Mercedes chassis of pre-1914 vintage. For the engine he took a six-cylinder 300-hp Maybach airship engine totalling no less than 23 litres, and with this car, in various forms, he won many events, often driving it on the road to and from races. Capable of nearly 130 mph, it was dangerous to drive and the Count crashed the car in 1922. Even at full speed the engine barely ticked over, which gave the car its distinctive sound and its name.

Zborowski's efforts then turned to Chittys 2 and 3, both comparative 'babies' with aircraft engines of only 18·8 litres and 14·7 litres respectively. These were built primarily for touring, and Chitty 2 took the Count safely on a Sahara safari.

Royale

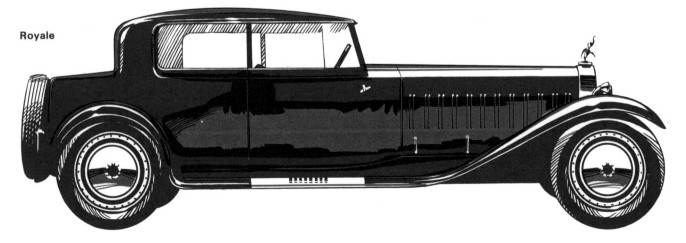

An earlier giant of Edwardian vintage carried the famous Napier name and was built originally for S. F. Edge to enter in the 1904 Gordon Bennett Race. Known as the L48, it had a 15·1-litre six-cylinder engine and only a two-speed gearbox. Its striking appearance was provided by the radiator, a series of tubes wrapped around each side of the huge engine. The car raced with moderate success for several years, and in 1907 Napier increased the stroke of the pistons to give an increased capacity of over 20 litres. In this form it scored several victories at Brooklands.

Royale was apt since only Royalty could afford it. Only three were sold, due to the financial collapse of 1929, but today the Royale is considered one of the most beautiful cars ever made. Big can be beautiful as well!

Of modern giants, one of the most interesting is the Rolls Royce built by Englishman John Dodd. This 'special' uses a 26-litre Rolls Royce Merlin

Babs

Giant of them all — Parry Thomas's Babs racer had a Liberty V12 aero engine totalling 27 litres. Thomas was killed attempting to better his own land speed record when the driving chain was thrown off after a wheel collapse.

Probably the most gigantic giant ever seen in the UK was Babs, a two-seat racer with a 27-litre V12 Liberty aero engine. This was another Zborowski project, and in its early days had several successes at Brooklands as the Higham Special. However, it was not until it passed into the hands of Parry Thomas in the mid-1920s that it achieved lasting fame as Babs. Thomas in fact broke the land speed record twice with this car in 1926 at around 170 mph, and in the following year lost his life in a further attempt at Pendine Sands in Wales when a rear wheel collapsed and flung the driving chain off its sprocket, killing Thomas instantly. The car was buried beneath the sands and lay there for many years until it was unearthed recently for probable restoration.

The name of Bugatti is famous for the familiar French blue sports racing cars of the 1920s and '30s. These were in no way giants, but in 1926/7 Ettore Bugatti set out to create the world's most illustrious road car — a giant with a 14-foot wheelbase and a 12·7-litre straight-eight engine. Known as the Royale, it had a 300-hp engine of very advanced engineering which was maintained free of charge for the life of its owner. Since the chassis alone was said to cost £100,000 in 1927, the name

engine from a Second World War Spitfire plane, mounted in a tough steel chassis. The engine is governed down to 2,500 rpm and coupled to a specially adapted Rolls Royce automatic gearbox. With this gearing the car is capable of 200 mph, although, since this is a road car, there are few opportunities to use the full potential! The bodywork was built up in fiberglass to provide a two-seat closed touring body, and apart from being much in demand for demonstrations etc, it is in regular use as a road vehicle by the owner, who also has two 'normal' Rolls Royces to keep it company!

Probably the largest private car in production, the Checker Aerobus Limousine seats 12, has a wheelbase of 189 ins and an overall length of 270 ins.

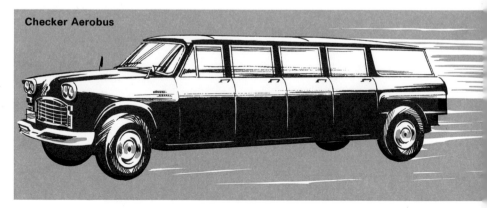

Checker Aerobus

Speed Records

The Jeantaud and Jenatzy electric racers

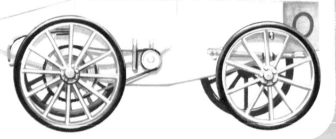

During 1899, two Frenchmen raised the land speed record several times in their electric racers — Jeantaud in his chain-driven model and Jenatzy in the torpedo-shaped Jamais Contente.

Segrave's 1,000-hp Sunbeam became the first to top 200 mph in 1927 with this big red monster powered by two V12 aircraft engines. It weighed four tons!

Earliest land speed records date from 1898, when Comte Gaston de Chasseloup-Laubat purred over the flying kilometer in his electric Jeantaud racer at 39·24 mph. During the following year, Laubat and Jenatzy, in another electric racer, between them raised the record five times, leaving it at 65·79 mph — despite dire warnings from the medical profession as to what might happen to the human body at such excessive speeds! Jenatzy's torpedo-shaped racer became the first to record the magic mile-a-minute and has the honor of being the last electric car to hold the land speed record.

Since then, many drivers in many weird and wonderful machines have gained or attempted to break the land speed record. Until 1964 the FIA (Federation Internationale Automobile) regulations laid down that to be eligible the machine had to have at least four wheels with two of them driven, and it was generally the case that to challenge the record one took the biggest engine or combination of engines available and installed them in a giant chassis. Many monster record holders have been powered by aircraft engines, often supercharged, but in 1928 American Frank Lockhart set out to prove that a good littl'un could beat a good big'un with his 3-litre Stutz Black Hawk. The engine was a V16 with a crank shaft and supercharger for each bank of cylinders. Lockhart also paid a good deal of attention to streamlining, with fully faired-in wheels and an almost completely smooth body. To do this he dispensed with the need for bulky radiators in the air-stream by using ice cooling in special surface containers. The attempt nearly worked, but was dogged by bad luck. On one run

Segrave's Sunbeam

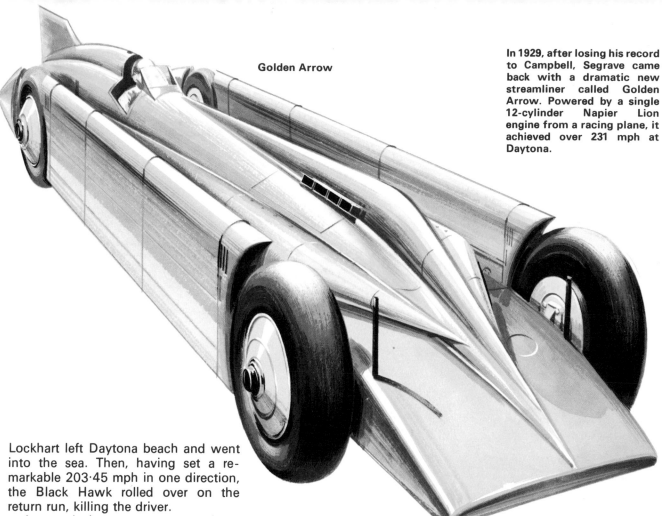

Golden Arrow

In 1929, after losing his record to Campbell, Segrave came back with a dramatic new streamliner called Golden Arrow. Powered by a single 12-cylinder Napier Lion engine from a racing plane, it achieved over 231 mph at Daytona.

Lockhart left Daytona beach and went into the sea. Then, having set a remarkable 203·45 mph in one direction, the Black Hawk rolled over on the return run, killing the driver.

As speeds rise, targets are passed and new ones set. After Jenatzy had bettered 60 mph, the next target was 100 mph: it was Louis Rigolly who covered the flying kilometer in his Gobron Brillié at 103·56 mph in July 1904. It took over 20 years, with the First World War intervening, for the next 50 mph to be achieved. Malcolm Campbell appeared in the record books for the first time in 1924 when he took his 350-hp V12 Sunbeam to 146·16 mph at Pendine Sands in North Wales. Then in 1925 he was back on the sands to run what by then was a rather ancient car to a new record of 150·87 mph.

Progress towards new targets from this point became more rapid with names like Campbell, Segrave and Parry Thomas exchanging places in the record books. Campbell went out with a Napier-based special in 1927 to record nearly 175 mph at Pendine, but almost immediately this was shattered in a big way by his rival, Sir Henry Segrave. On March 29, 1927, Segrave's twin-engined 1,000-hp Sunbeam thundered across Daytona beach in Florida to record a two-way average of 203·79 mph. On the same beach in the following year, Campbell took back the record with

206·96 mph with the Napier special before beginning his famous line of Bluebirds in which he was to break the 250 and 300 mph barriers.

It was the Frenchman Louis Rigolly who was first to top 100 mph in 1904, driving a 13½-litre four-cylinder Gobron Brillié.

Gobron Brillié

19

Stanley steamer

Arfons' Green Monster

Apart from electric cars, steam cars were early holders of the land speed record. In 1906, Fred Marriott drove the American Stanley steamer to a record of 121·57 mph.

Art Arfons joined Breedlove in a record-breaking duel in 1964/65, and between them they raised the record from 400 to 600 mph. Arfons' Green Monster, like Breedlove's car, was powered by a J79 jet engine from a Hustler bomber. Arfons' best record was 576·55 mph in 1965.

Goldenrod

Goldenrod, built by the American Summers Bros, is the holder of the wheel-driven land speed record at 409·27 mph.

American Frank Lockhart challenged for the record in 1928 with a mere 3-litre car — the Stutz Black Hawk. Although it managed over 200 mph, Lockhart was killed in the attempt.

In 1932 his supercharged Napier aero-engined Bluebird averaged 253·968 mph for the record at Daytona. Three years later, in a new Bluebird powered by a Rolls Royce racing aero engine, he passed the 300 mph mark at Bonneville Salt Flats in Utah, and averaged the two-way flying mile course at 304·311 mph. This was the last time that Sir Malcolm's name appeared in the record books, and it was

left to George Eyston and John Cobb to push for new records until the Second World War intervened.

In 1938 John Cobb in his Railton special recorded 350·2 mph at Bonneville, bettered by Eyston in the same year. It was Cobb, however, who left the record standing at 369·70 mph in 1939 before hostilities began.

After the war it was Cobb again who rekindled interest in the land speed record when in 1947 he took the teardrop-shaped Railton Mobil Special to Bonneville and just missed the magic 400 mph with a record of 394.20 mph in a car powered by two Napier Lion aero engines of now almost vintage years.

Cobb's record was to stand for many years, mainly through lack of interest and the finance to build what was a very costly machine with dubious benefits at a time when the world was recovering from a war.

But during the 1960s the name of Campbell emerged again in the shape of Sir Malcolm's son Donald. With his father's mechanic and designer, Leo Villa, he built a new Bluebird to try for

Stutz Black Hawk

20

the record, using a Bristol Proteus turbine aero engine. However, before he had a chance to prove the car he was eclipsed by American Craig Breedlove who, flaunting the rules, sped across Bonneville in a three-wheeler jet-powered device at 407·45 mph. Record-breaking machines were supposed to have at least four wheels and be driven through the wheels, but Breedlove was the fastest man on the earth and the whole world knew it.

Donald Campbell's undoubted achievement in 1964, when he took the official record at 403·10 mph at Lake Eyre, Australia, had a rather hollow ring to it. There has been talk of reviving Bluebird again to try for the wheel-driven record, but it will not carry a Campbell name. Like his father, Donald also gave his energies to the water speed record and was killed on Coniston Water during a record attempt.

Although the age of the jet-powered record holder had arrived, the wheel-driven record was raised again in 1965 by the American Summers brothers. After a long period of records held by aero-engined cars, the Summers Bros snatched the record with Goldenrod, powered by four Chrysler piston engines, developed from passenger car motors. Goldenrod's four gasoline-injected engines totalled just under 28 litres and developed around 2,400 hp. Perhaps their record of 409·27 mph will stand for ever, since most interest is now centered around the jet-powered machines which have new records of their own and new targets to break.

1964/65 was an intense period of record breaking with Breedlove being joined by the Arfons brothers in a battle for supremacy. Art Arfons took the Green Monster to over 634 mph in 1964, and in the same year Breedlove returned to Bonneville with Spirit of America to clock 468 mph and then to pass the 500 mph mark with 526·28 mph. Arfons

wasn't to be outdone, and still in 1964 he raised the record to 536·71 mph in a device powered by a General Electric J79 jet engine from a Hustler bomber. Back came Breedlove in 1965 with a new J79-powered machine – Spirit of America Sonic 1 – to swap records with Arfons several times before Breedlove cracked a new target – 600·60 mph.

Things quietened down after this until in 1970 the Natural Gas Corporation of America backed a new project powered by liquid fuel – similar to that used in the US space program. Reaction Dynamics devised a four-wheeled projectile around this rocket motor and dragster driver Gary Gabelich was contracted to try to take the record. He did – at 631·36 mph.

It's hard to see any reason why anyone should try to break this record. The sheer enormity of the cost cannot be justified in terms of research or publicity. But no doubt someone will try.

Malcolm Campbell features several times in the record books, and it was he who broke both the 250 and 300 mph barriers in his Bluebird machine. This 304·311 mph record breaker was powered by a single Rolls racing aero engine.

It was American Craig Breedlove who shook up record breaking in 1963/64 with his jet-powered cars. It was Breedlove who first topped 400 mph and then 500 mph with his three-wheeler Spirit of America.

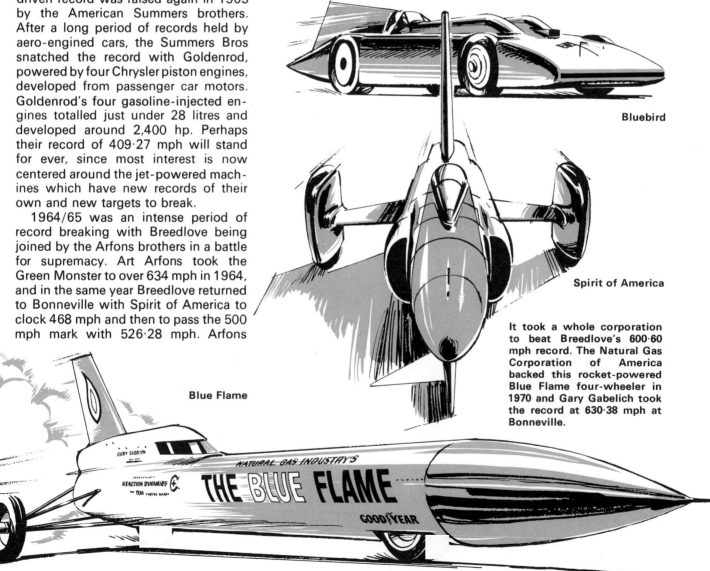

Bluebird

Spirit of America

Blue Flame

It took a whole corporation to beat Breedlove's 600·60 mph record. The Natural Gas Corporation of America backed this rocket-powered Blue Flame four-wheeler in 1970 and Gary Gabelich took the record at 630·38 mph at Bonneville.

Wheels Across the Water

Orukter Amphibolos

on the ground, had more success with a canoe-shaped car which he named Ravailler. Powered by a 20-hp engine, it made its maiden trip in 1907 and was sufficiently successful for its backers to take it to America for exhibition purposes.

Germany during the 1930s was a hot-bed of engineering development, and it was here that Hans Trippel began developing a successful line of practical amphibians. In 1932 he produced his first car, and two years later it was in production for the rich hunting, shooting and fishing market. It had four-wheel drive on land and used a propeller when in the water. Then, with the outbreak of war, there were military Trippels in

Earliest attempt at an amphibian was a steam-driven craft with the unlikely name of Orukter Amphibolos. It floated – even at 20 tons weight – but the wheels collapsed on land!

Over the years, many people have tried to devise transport that served more than one purpose. A car that had clip-on wings for conversion to a plane was once devised, but more successful, and more practical, have been amphibians in various forms. Some have been more or less for recreational use only, but others have had a proven record as multi-purpose military vehicles.

Perhaps the original amphibian was built in the age of steam – in 1805 in Philadelphia, Penn. The Orukter Amphibolos, as it was fancifully named, was a flat-bottomed steam barge equipped with wheels and axles, one of which was driven via belts from the steam engine when on land. It apparently worked on water, but when asked to tackle land travel the wheels collapsed under its reported 20 ton weight.

Some 70 years later, an inventive Frenchman, with his feet more firmly

Attempts have been made to convert existing vehicles as amphibians. This version of the Land Rover used four huge floatation tires for both buoyancy and drive.

Perhaps the most famous of all amphibians – the Second World War DUKW, or Duck as it's best known. Many of these personnel carriers are still in use all over the world.

Floating Land Rover

service, many of them produced at the captured Bugatti works in French Alsace Lorraine.

Better known than the Trippel is the Schwimmwagen, one of many versions of the famous German Volkswagen. Schwimmwagen means simply 'swim-vehicle,' and mechanically it was similar to the 'people-car' with a rear-mounted air-cooled engine but with additional

DUKW

ATV

drive to the front wheels. Drive in the water was through an ingenious propeller out-drive which swung down to engage with a short shaft from the engine. About 14,000 of these amphibians were produced and many are still serviceable.

Best known amphibian is the Second World War DUKW, or Duck as it is better known. Based on the American Jeep chassis, it had twin-propeller drive in the water and played a big part in Allied landings in many parts of the globe. Still in commission is the British Alvis Stalwart, built by the very famous builders of luxury touring cars in Coventry. In military trim it is powered by a 6·5-litre Rolls Royce engine which drives all six wheels, the front four of which steer on both land and water. In the water it is powered by water jets.

In the early 1960s, Hans Trippel's name cropped up again. He designed and built the Eurocar, or Amphicar, of which several thousand were made. Based on Triumph Herald 1200 components, it had an open fiber-glass body

and drive to two propellers mounted under the finned tail. It was possible to drive down to the water on the road wheels, down a ramp and immediately engage the propellers. Speed through the water was about 6 mph, while on land it could easily top 70. Front wheels did the steering on land and water.

It was a fun car and several are still in use in the UK by owners who live near the water.

A modern military amphibian – the Alvis Stalwart, which is driven through all six wheels by a Rolls Royce engine and powered when afloat by powerful water jets.

ATV – all terrain vehicle – the modern way to go amphibian. Fat 'doughnut' tires cope with any land surface and provide traction through the water, although a small outboard motor can be used as an auxiliary.

23

The weird Phanomobil three-wheeler looked lethal and probably was to drive, but fulfilled the need for cheap, reliable transport in Germany, around 1910.

Economy Cars

Phanomobil

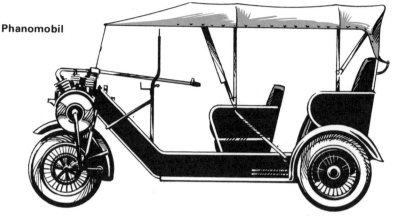

Ugly-bug Fairthorpe Atom appeared in 1955 and featured fiber-glass tear-drop body with 2-plus seating. Three BSA motorcycle engines were used, from 250 cc–650 cc, the latter capable of 75 mph, thanks to the aerodynamics.

Also in 1910, the British AC company produced the three-wheeled Sociable, with single rear wheel. Sold for five years at under $250 – even the army bought them.

There has been a need for economical cars ever since the turn of the century. However affluent society becomes there are people who need transport that is cheap to buy, cheap to run – even if only as a second or third car. Sometimes, too, social and economic pressures stimulate additional demand for economy cars, as in the years following the two World Wars. And today, with fuel prices rising, economy cars are once again becoming fashionable on both cost and ecological grounds. Naturally, some of the attempts to achieve economy have been fairly hilarious, odd, or just plain nonsensical.

The German 1910 Phanomobil was certainly odd looking, although apparently it was reliable and economical to run. In appearance it resembled a home-made golf cart and could be bought in two- or four-seat forms, neither of which offered the occupants anything in the way of protection. All the working bits were suspended over the single front wheel – a Vee-twin air-cooled engine, cooled by a fan, of

Fairthorpe atom

880 cc capacity. There were two forward speeds and the wheel was driven by a chain. It all looks fairly lethal, stuck out there in front – and indeed the driver might well have agreed since he had to turn the whole thing through a bend with just a tiller bar.

In England there was more vogue at that time for econocars, and in 1910 the AC company were producing an economical oddity of their own called the Sociable. This three-wheeler had its 631-cc air-cooled single cylinder in the center, driving the single rear wheel by chain. The appearance is a little like an overgrown push-chair, but with two

AC Sociable

24

d'Yrsan three-wheeler

French d'Yrsan followed Morgan three-wheeler practice with single wheel at back, engine forward. This sporty model, which was produced between 1923 and 1930, packed a 1-litre Ruby engine.

Three wheels and 2·6 litres was America's idea of economy in 1948. The Davis car had four seats — side by side.

Davis three-wheeler

seats side by side. It had tiller steering on the two front wheels and in most respects was very basic, although items such as small windshield, hood and protective apron could be had as extras. It did the job, though, and was certainly economical at under $250 basic throughout its fairly long life. There was even a version for the military, carrying a machine-gun!

America has only recently started to become concerned about economy, but in 1948 there was one curious attempt at an econocar — the Californian Davis company produced an extraordinary three-wheeler with a 2·6-litre engine (which was economical by American standards). Its torpedo-like coupé body had a single wheel at the front and seating for four — all abreast. Their performance figures were always rather less than claimed, but it did manage 75 mph (not the claimed 100) at 28 mpg.

Three-wheelers have often been popular for economy — the Reliant Robin and Bond Bug are current examples — and were especially popular during the 1920s. The British Morgan concern made three-wheelers from Edwardian times right through to the post-Second World War period, and the Morgan had its imitators in several countries. The French d'Yrsan was a typical example and several versions were made including an eccentrically streamlined model developed for competition. The semi-elliptic bodywork was interrupted only by the bonnet and the hatch for the pilot, but with a water-cooled four-cylinder engine of 972 cc the d'Yrsan was capable of speeds in the 70s. A supercharged 1,100-cc version was also used in racing, and 85 mph was its respectable top speed.

In the mid-1950s, several odd econocars were tried, including the bubble cars (pages 30–31). A particularly hideous attempt was the 1955 Fairthorpe Atom with a tear-drop body making full

use of the new freedom of fiber-glass construction. Three engines were available, all BSA motorcycle units — 250, 350 and 650 cc. There was a small space behind the two front seats for one small adult or two children.

The Morgan three-wheeler, built in 1914, was produced in an attempt to popularize the motor vehicle by reducing fuel consumption and lowering costs.

Morgan three-wheeler

Fast & Furious

Priddle's 'funny car'

Top UK drag racer Dennis Priddle has a two-car team, racing both an AA-fuel 'rail' and a 'funny car' designed around a Chrysler Avenger body. Both cars use supercharged and injected American V8 engines, around 1,400 hp a-piece.

Between modified production cars and 'funny cars' are the 'competition altereds,' using recognizable car bodies but with chassis and engine open to anything. This UK-built 'altered' uses a Ford Model T body and fuel-injected Chevrolet engine.

Many people think that motor sport is becoming very dull as mechanical sophistication takes more and more drama out of Formula One racing, and legislation reduces the opportunity to road-race or rally. One form of motor sport, however, is really catching on all over the world after becoming the number one sport in the United States — drag racing.

Simply, drag racing involves pairs of vehicles competing with each other over a standing start quarter mile, and if that seems fairly dull, the sight and sounds of drag racing are quite the opposite.

The name of the game is acceleration, and originally it began on the streets of America as the owners of hot-rods — modified road cars — staged impromptu standing-start races away from the traffic lights. Cars in America have generally been modified mainly for acceleration, due partly to the fact that their big V8 engines could be easily adjusted to give shattering power, and partly to the fact that there is less need in America to develop the suspension for cornering

since roads are generally straighter than in Europe.

The term 'drag racing' came from racing down the 'main drag' — the main street — but it was frowned on by the police, and gradually, through the 1950s, drag racing became organized off the highway on purpose-built 'strips.'

Early drag racing machinery tended to be modified street machinery and a few specials, and in a sense this has not changed in that it is still possible for the owner of a 'hot' street car to go down to the nearest drag strip and compete. But what has happened, of course, is the development of specialized drag racing machinery built to cover that quarter mile in the shortest possible time.

A pure dragster has the most powerful engine possible, the lightest chassis, and the sketchiest body. It's known as a 'rail,' from the days when a dragster was stripped to the chassis rails. Now it has a long, skinny frame, often over 240 inches long and only as wide as the driver. Early rails had the driver sitting over the rear axle with the engine almost between his legs, but in the late 1960s top drivers like American Don Garlits pioneered the rear-engined car and virtually all top dragsters now are rear- or mid-engined. It's safer for the driver,

'Competition altereds'

There are categories for lesser powered rails too — the unsupercharged ones that run on gasoline, with smaller capacity engines etc. In the UK there tends to be more variety, since classes have sprung up around native engines.

Consistently one of the top 'funny car' drivers in the States, Don 'The Shoe' Schumacher set trends in the ultra-low Wonder wagon. The body is a lengthened, narrowed and lowered replica of a Chevrolet Vega. Underneath lurks a full AA-fuel 1,600-hp engine.

Wonder wagon

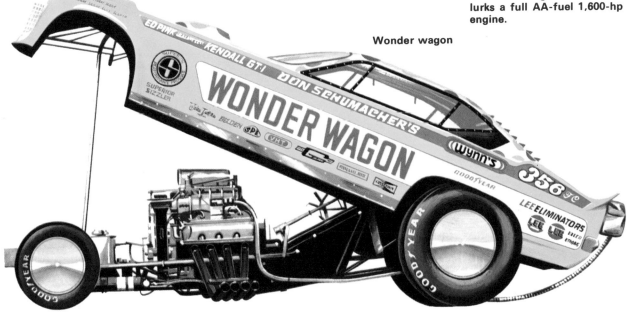

too, since clutch, supercharger or complete engine explosions are common.

Top drag drivers on a good track cover the quarter mile in under 6 seconds in America, around 6·5 seconds in the UK. The acceleration is shattering, of course, as is the top speed at the end of the run — over 220 mph! Some drivers have crossed the finish line at over 240 mph. How do they stop from these speeds? By releasing exotic parachutes!

If you watch a drag race you'll notice that those low, fat rear tires 'grow' with the centrifugal force of the acceleration, providing a novel way of raising the gearing as speed increases.

The AA-fuellers are the quickest, but there are many other classes in drag racing. Popular with the crowds are the 'funny cars' which resemble production cars, though they are nothing more than ultra-light fiber-glass shells on a short version of a full-blown dragster. They are known for their burn-outs and the sight of two wildly-painted 'funny cars,' with their back ends wreathed in smoke as they scream out of the 'bleach box,' is something not to be forgotten. In their most developed form, 'funny cars' use the same engines as the AA dragsters and their times over the quarter mile are almost as quick, although they have yet to better 6 seconds.

Dragsters have been built using 1,000-cc Mini and Ford engines, and one driver, John Whitmore, consistently runs low 9 second times in his tiny supercharged rail — powered by a modified Morris 1000 engine — quicker than some V8-engined machines. Some intrepid drivers go drag racing in go-karts, again beating many larger engined machines in the process.

But apart from the exotic specials, participation is still very strong and the street car element of drag racing has remained very important. In America local events have a huge proportion of street entries when owners drive to the strip and 'run what they brung' to keep alive the original grudge element from the sport's early days.

'Run what you brung' — this fine Swedish 'hot rod' drives around on the road, but can also cut some very quick times on the drag strip. It's based on a 1932 Plymouth coupé with modern Chevrolet engine.

Swedish 'hot rod'

Bubble Cars

Brutsch Mopetta

Brutsch Mopetta was interesting but unexciting with only a 49-cc engine and styling that looked a little like a carnival car.

Bond was a pioneer of bubble cars in the UK. Original design was very spartan with single-cylinder chain-driven engine over the front wheel. To start it involved pulling a string, like a lawn mower, and suspension relied on air in the tires. The latest bubble car carrying the Bond name is the futuristic Bug, designed for young enthusiasts.

The bubble car was one of those phenomena which suddenly emerged to cater for a particular motoring need at a particular time. The idea was not especially new — low cost motoring was the aim — but the form it took was peculiar to the 1950s. The need arose during the early '50s for vehicles which were cheap to buy and cheap to run as Europe started to recover from the war. People were starting to demand the mobility of their own transport, but the cost of new cars was still relatively high in comparison to wages. So a new era of economy cars was needed and it was the production methods and the styling fads of the time that gave the cars their rounded shapes and the tag 'bubble cars.'

One of the best known bubble cars carried a very famous name — that of the German aircraft maker Messerschmidt — and it was perhaps this machine that gave the bubbles their name. Messerschmidts were made from 1953 to 1960 in various forms, all of which had two seats, one behind the other, and a perspex bubble canopy like a Second World War plane. Originally the car was made with three wheels, two at the front, but later versions had a four-wheel layout and a 500-cc Sachs engine instead of the 175-cc and 200-cc engines in the three-wheelers. Driving was unusual, with steering through a small horse shoe-shaped wheel which had very limited movement and high gearing.

The Germans, with the Messerschmidt, the BMW Isetta and the Heinkel had most success in the bubble car market. One German make that didn't make its mark, however, was the Brutsch, whose founders seemed very strong on

Peel

producing prototypes but weak on getting them into production. Their 49-cc Mopetta of 1956 vintage had the distinction of being one of the smallest cars ever at 5 feet 7 inches long, but was

Bond Bug

Messerschmidt Tiger

Odd but successful, the German Messerschmidt had the original 'bubble' canopy covering two seats, one behind the other. This is the four-wheel 500-cc Tiger version, made in 1959.

not a success. Its single seat three-wheel body perhaps too closely resembled a carnival car!

Probably the original UK bubble car was designed by Laurie Bond in 1951. Bond's Minicar was ingenious, if rudimentary, and had a single wheel at the front driven by a 122-cc motorcycle engine above. The Minicar was refined and improved over a period of many years, and in its final form it bowed out in 1965. Along the way it had acquired suspension, front-wheel braking, more powerful engines, and four seats. Bond was among the first in the UK to use fiber-glass for production bodywork too.

In 1969 Bond was taken over by the Reliant concern, who also made (and still make) a lightweight fiber-glass three-wheeler, and the Minicar was dropped in favor of a brand new design called the Bond Bug, designed by Ogle Associates and using the Reliant four-stroke engine for power. The Bug is aimed very much at the young fun-car market and is very striking looking with a wedge-shaped body, flip-up canopy for entry, and a chopped-off tail which incorporates a blackboard so that the owner can express his message to the world as he goes along! It's a striking car, and because of its light weight it has a good performance. Bond Bugs come in any color as long as it's orange!

Did you realise that the Isle of Man once had a car industry? In the early 1960s the Peel bubble car was produced at Peel, IOM — a little three-wheeled single-seater powered by a 49-cc two-stroke engine. Overall it measured just 4 feet 5 inches, although a later version had two seats in tandem. It was an interesting try, and in today's climate of opinion favoring small economical town cars, the smart little Peel might well have done better. It was interesting too that the company tried an electric version of the car.

The French, with their fine traditions in odd-ball small cars, produced one outstanding novelty. Called the Reyonnah, it was a little like the Messerschmidt in appearance in that it had two seats in tandem. It had four wheels, the rear pair very close together; the front wheels were made to fold underneath the car so that in the closed position the front was no wider than the rear. It was a very clever idea, but there was really little point in a folding car so not many were made.

Produced in the Isle of Man, the single-seat Peel was only 4 feet 5 inches long. Today it might find favor as a city car.

French Reyonnah looked like a Messerschmidt — front wheels folded underneath to same width as rear pair. A pointless novelty.

Reyonnah

Dream Cars

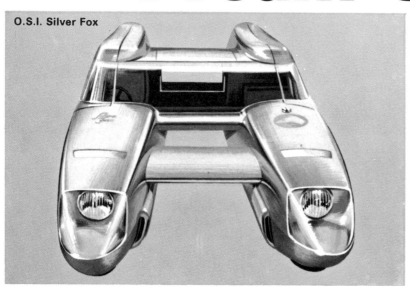

O.S.I. Silver Fox

Built at Turin, Italy, the O.S.I. Silver Fox's carefully calculated lines make for the very minimum in drag when travelling at speed.

Hard Hat Hauler features construction workers' equipment, including a huge protective helmet in polished alloy. The engine has three superchargers.

If there's any one class of car that really earns the title of 'weird' it's the dream cars — cars that are the ultimate, whether in speed, looks, facilities or whatever. The difficulty in selecting vehicles for this chapter is simply that some cars are more of a nightmare than a dream. But there's no accounting for taste — an enthusiast whose dream revolves

around an ultra-streamlined body packed with *the* most powerful engine may be left quite cold by a motor-minded cowboy's visions of a car that has a saddle instead of a seat and goes 'moo' when you press the horn. Equally, the cowboy might be baffled by the motoring veteran who longs to take the wheel of the original Model T Ford.

Some dreams have, of course, come true. A number of private individuals have actually built the magnificent motors which for so long have haunted their waking hours. And many car manufacturers, with many thousands of dollars to spare, have pumped cash into their idea of a dream car. In the case of the car companies, such a venture is often basically a publicity stunt — something to draw attention to their workmanship at the world's motor shows. With its gleaming paintwork and sparkling, chromium-plated engine, the 'dream car' really is something for the motor maniacs to feast their eyes and imaginations on. The irony of such a situation is that the car, in all probability, doesn't actually go. It looks good, feels good (if you're allowed to touch it!) —

Hard Hat Hauler

but it would never move so much as a piston, simply because it wasn't built to go . . . just to be!

However, there are exceptions to every rule, and one very dreamy one is the O.S.I. Silver Fox. Based on a 'twin-boom' design, this neat piece of automotive engineering is powered by a one-litre Gordini engine. There is seating room for one only, unfortunately; the second pontoon (on the right as you look at it) houses the engine.

A very different kind of dream is the George Barris-built Hard Hat Hauler. Produced from a nutty model idea, this hot-rod-based anomaly incorporates features from the construction world. The basis of the machine is a hot-rod chassis with a replica 1923 Model T Ford body. The roof, if you can call it that, is a 4-foot highly

which its originators had for it were never realized.

The car was built by Enrico Nardi on the commission of a sporting gentleman named Damonte, who planned to race it in the 1955 Le Mans, together with a friend named Crovetto. It was these Frenchmen who laid down the design for the Nardi, which, like the Silver Fox, was based on the twin-boom principle widely used in machines built for record-breaking attempts. These booms, or fuselages, were bridged by a shallow center section which housed the radiator – skilfully merged into the smooth lines of the body – and a 'seat.' This seat, which was nothing more than a small compartment in the center panel, alongside the driver, was required by the Le Mans regulations, which stated that a second seat should

PF Modulo – from the makers of some of the world's dreamiest cars, Ferrari.

Ferrari, PF Modulo

polished alloy replica of a construction worker's helmet, while behind the driver is a giant 'lunch box' to hold gas tank and battery. At the front Barris mounted a fork-lift truck assembly, behind which lurks a chrome and polished V8 engine, capped by no fewer than three massive superchargers. Every detail has been attended to for the dreamy world of the show car circuit – even the chassis is chromed and highly polished!

Ferrari is a name that has become synonymous with the phrase 'dream car' and their PF Modulo doesn't need any sales talk to convince you that it *is* a dream. Housed within this beautiful piece of streamlining is a rear-mounted 4-stroke engine of 5,000 cc. It has a 5-speed fully synchronized gear-box, independent suspension, and is fitted with disc brakes. In case you're wondering if it would fit in Dad's garage, the PF Modulo is 176·38 inches long, 80·63 inches wide and just 32·83 inches high.

Some dreams, sadly, never come true – and although the Nardi 750 cc racing car *was* built and *did* race, the hopes

be available for a theoretical passenger. Not missing a trick, the Frenchmen suggested that the lid to this seat might be used as an air brake!

The Nardi certainly looked the part of the dream car (although 'dreams' have become rather sleeker since 1955!), but it gave a disappointing performance at Le Mans, retiring early. Little more was heard of it after that.

Coming back to 'the dreams that don't go,' it isn't only the car manufacturers who build beautiful machines

A dream that *didn't* come true – the 750 cc Nardi. Although capable of around 108 mph in 1955, this 880-lb car never won a race or broke any records.

Nardi, 750 cc

Bathtub Buggy

Fastest bathroom in the West – Bathtub Buggy incorporates all luxury bathroom fittings in a wild hot-rod concept.

that will never be driven. On the American show car circuit there are many creations which are put together just for the sake of spectacle – and to earn money for their makers! In theory, of course, these zany motors ought to work, following as they do car or hot-rod practice. But there is never any intention of them coming to life; their engines, etc. have no 'innards.'

But even if they did go, can you imagine who would want to be seen driving them? Who, for instance, would have the nerve to take the Bathtub Buggy out for a spin? This George Barris creation is little more than a chassis with a dummy V8 engine on which has been mounted almost every bathroom fitting you can imagine. The driver (if there were one) is supposed to conduct the machine from a vanity seat, behind which is a genuine French bathtub, and above which is a sculpted brass shower unit.

Barris mounted the ornate wash basin in front of the radiator (instant hot water?) and the deck of the chassis is covered in gold porcelain tiles. The rest of the bathroom paraphernalia is

dotted around the machine – toilet paper, foot rests, lighted theatrical make-up mirror, Grecian style wall lights, etc. Even the exhaust system is 'plumbed in.' For enthusiasts who really like the idea of mobile hygiene, a model kit firm turned out 1/24th scale replicas of the Bathtub Buggy. A sort of dream come true – in miniature.

A bathroom on wheels is one thing, but if you saw a can of soup on wheels, you really *would* think you were dreaming – and having a bad dream at that! But in America *anything* is possible . . . and there *is* a can of soup on wheels. Again custom builder George Barris was the man behind this weird novelty car, but it begins to make sense when you know that Barris designed the vehicle for the Campbell Soup Company. The body of the car is modelled on a Campbell's can and to make sure everybody gets the advertiser's message, actual labelled cans are fitted to the wheel hubs – and there's even one fitted on the gear shift-knob. For additional 'flavor,' Barris had vegetables painted on the sides of the car, and on the seat.

With the overall look of a sporty roadster, and a Boss Mustang engine that really goes, this unique publicity car has two tanks stowed away inside its body — one is for high-octane gas . . . the other is for low calorie vegetable juice. All in all, the Campbell Roadster is what you might call a 'souped-up' job!

While on the subject of mobile food and publicity stunts, one wonders if anybody has ever thought of mobilizing that great edible epitome of the American way of life, the hamburger. The answer is 'yes'! And the builder was George Barris. Getting a gigantic hamburger on to wheels could, as you can imagine, cause problems. For example, where would the driver sit without getting covered in tomato catsup? And wouldn't the onions get in the way when you're trying to find the clutch? Barris found that the answer was to keep the hamburger well out of the driver's reach — by mounting it on the roof . . . or rather, mounting it *as* the roof!

The vehicle was intended as a mobile attraction for a hamburger restaurant chain, so Barris decided that a powered golf cart would be the ideal basis for such a gimmick. With the name of the restaurant splashed on the side of the cart and the replica hamburger supported above the driver's head, the message is clear and plain. As for being a dream — well, it might be more of a nightmare for hamburger-crazy people of a nervous disposition. Who'd believe the delicate kid who bursts into the house, declaring, 'Hey, Mom, I was chased all the way home by a five foot-wide hamburger!'

On a more macaber note, Boothill Express (seen below) was allegedly built from an original horse-drawn hearse by Ray Farhner, which explains the odd driving position, stage-coach style, over the flimsy front wheels. The huge rear wheels give the device its sharply raked appearance to emphasize what would be the power of the Chrysler dragster engine — if it worked. The 'dead' engine sits appropriately enough in the glass-sided coffin compartment with the eight chrome stacks for the dummy fuel injection poking through the roof. Paintwork is dusted with gold and highlighted with gold leaf.

Boothill Express was designed around a horsedrawn hearse, hence the stagecoach look to the driver's platform. Pony power is provided by dummy dragster engine.

Boothill Express

Movie Cars

Genevieve, the famous 1904 Darracq which starred in the film of the same name. The film, which featured Kenneth More and told the story of the London to Brighton race, helped stir up fresh interest in old cars all over the world.

Genevieve

The Alien – built for TV's time travelling Doctor Who. Although designed like a space ship, the Alien is actually registered for the road and can achieve over 100 mph from its tuned rear-mounted Chrysler Imp engine.

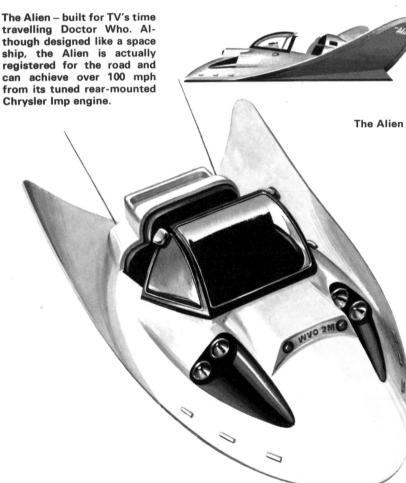

The Alien

The car industry and the film industry, both products of the 20th century, have grown up very much together, so it's natural that cars should feature very much in films past and present. Chaplin, Laurel and Hardy, and the Keystone Cops all used cars to great comic effect — they fell to pieces, exploded, were cut in two by circular saws and were subject to all manner of tricks to keep the audiences laughing in the days of the 'silent' movies.

Films have been made *around* cars too — remember the veteran Darracq in *Genevieve*? Or the vintage Bentley in *The Fast Lady*? Or, more recently, the Disney films featuring Volkswagen Beetles in *The Love Bug* and *Herbie Rides Again*?

Car sequences as part of the dramatic action are legion. Virtually every James Bond film features either weird machines or exciting chases — or a combination of both, as in *Diamonds are Forever*. The car chase in the Steve McQueen film *Bullitt* is a classic, while that in *The French Connection* runs it a close second.

One of the best known movie cars is probably Chitty Chitty Bang Bang. In the next chapter on 'The Giants' you'll see the original Chittys built for wealthy Edwardian racer Count Zborowski, but the film Chitty is the creation of James

James Bond moon buggy

Bond writer Ian Fleming, who wrote a children's adventure story around a mythical car carrying the same name. This Chitty — or these Chittys, since in fact six were built for the film — had magical properties. It could fly, float, hover, and of course do amazing things on land for its owners. It could act as a magic carpet which could fly to faraway fairytale castles, rescue children from the grip of evil barons — in fact there wasn't much it couldn't do! Although made to look like an authentic Edwardian tourer, the modern Chitty was dummied up around a modern Ford V8 engine with automatic transmission. Details like the huge exhaust pipes were in fact just for show. As for flying? All done by trick photography! But that's 'magic,' of a sort!

The James Bond films have spawned a variety of amazing machines, most of which did not appear in the original Ian Fleming thrillers. There was the Aston Martin DB6 that had an ejector seat, guns which appeared from nowhere and a host of other novelties designed to enable Bond to come out on top of whatever encounter he might have with the 'baddies.'

In *Diamonds are Forever*, Bond stumbles upon an astronaut's training ground and conveniently makes his escape in a moon buggy across the

Nevada desert. The brainchild of film designer Ken Adam, the moon buggy was made in California by a well-known builder of extraordinary custom machinery called Dean Jeffries (he designed and built another film car, the Monkeemobile, used by the Monkees pop and comedy group). Based on an engine and transaxle assembly from a rear-engined Corvair passenger car, the moon buggy can actually drive around at up to 80 mph, although at that speed it's pretty hair-raising! The steering is carried out by a small tiller geared to the steering box (from an Austin Healey Sprite) so that even the smallest movement on the tiller means a considerable turn at the wheels. The axles have been extended so that the width of the vehicle is the same as the length — 14 feet. The tires look like real 'moon walkers,' but in fact they are merely old dragster tires with slices cut out to make them resemble cross-country tracks.

That well-known time traveller Doctor Who has driven through his TV series in a variety of oddities, including a mock Edwardian runabout. Another form of transport takes him into the future in a landborne flying saucer. Although it appears to hover, The Alien, as it's called, is really a three-wheeler and was built to be used legally on the roads of Britain. At the back is the engine and transmission from a Hillman Imp saloon car, used with Imp suspension. At the front is a single Mini wheel suspended on parts from the Bond Bug three-wheeler. The body is intended to look like something from outer space and was built up in fiber-glass with a metalflake paint finish in silver and red. It weighs only 14 cwt all told, which gives The Alien a top speed of over 100 mph. No, it doesn't fly!

The James Bond movies have spawned several odd machines, including this mocked-up moon buggy from *Diamonds are Forever*. Though odd to drive, the buggy was built to work and is capable of tearing overland at over 70 mph. Californian car builder Dean Jeffries was paid over $20,000 to construct it.

James Bond author Ian Fleming created a mythical Chitty Chitty Bang Bang car for a children's adventure story. It could fly, float, hover and do amazing deeds on the road. In all, six Chittys were built for the film version.

Chitty Chitty Bang Bang

The Specials

offshoots of the off-road craze. The first beach buggy, or dune buggy, appeared in California and has since been copied in many parts of the world. Most buggies are based on a Volkswagen chassis, which is a good base for an off-road vehicle since it has the engine and transmission at the rear, where it can be most effective on loose ground. To make the machine more manoeuvrable on rugged ground, the floor pan of the VW is shortened by 10-14 inches, and wide wheels and tires are fitted to cope

VW Racing buggy

Developed from VW dune buggies, specially built single-seat racing buggies are quick and manoeuvrable. VW or Porsche power is still used, but the chassis is a special, tough space-frame.

As restrictions on the roads of the world increase, and as people have more leisure time to use, there has been a movement to get off the road and get away from it all. This has bred the development of special off-road vehicles, and in turn this has led to various forms of racing using even greater extremes of machinery.

In America particularly, where there are open deserts available for exploration, wide beaches and dunes, a whole new breed of machines has developed, some just purely for fun, some for more practical use, and others for the long and tortuous races held on these terrains.

The beach buggy is one of the nuttiest

with the rough going. Replacing the standard VW Beetle bodywork is a lightweight open fiber-glass shell, usually with only two seats, though four-seat buggies have been made. The body looks a little like a shapely bathtub with a skirt around the rim just to cover the wheels and the engine.

Many buggies are used on the roads as cheap fun vehicles, especially in the UK where there is little truly open land where a buggy can be used.

More specialized versions of the dune buggy are now common in the United States, still using VW engines but often now with specially constructed steel tube frames instead of the rather flimsy flat floor pan of the car. This is the kind of machine that competes in the off-road races, like the Baja 1000 and 500, the Dam 400 and other tough terrain races of endurance.

A more familiar beach or dune buggy which was developed for recreational sand terrain in California; it has since been copied all over the world. This attractive UK version is used on the road.

Beach Buggy

Fitted with highly modified VW or Porsche engines, the lightweight space-frame one- or two-seat buggies are ideal for sand, rocks or almost any terrain. Rear tires are usually very chunky with deep, wide treads for grip; front wheels are narrow with simple, grooved tread around the circumference for steering grip on loose ground. The buggies are a spectacular sight as they leap over rough ground, often with all four wheels in the air.

A new breed of off-road machine is the VW Baja-Bug. Basically a VW car modified for off-road use, these Bugs can also be used on the road, since the main working parts and body are retained. Baja-Bugs have chopped-off front and rear bodywork for lightness and manoeuvrability, toughened suspension and off-road wheels and tires. Engines, of course, can be modified to the same extent as their space-frame brethren. Although very much VW Beetles underneath, Baja-Bugs look very dramatic with their short, wide, chunky stance, fat wheels and the exposed engine at the rear. It's also quite easy to modify a perfectly ordinary road machine to look like a Baja-Bug, even if it will never leave the tarmac!

VW Baja Bug

There are several utility vehicles already made for rough and tumble use— the Land Rover, Jeep and Toyota Land Cruiser are the best known — but in America there is a class of utility vehicle for the recreation market which is designed to be easy to drive on the road with car type comfort, yet with scope for driving overland, hauling boats, trailers etc at the weekend.

Spectacular VW Baja-Bug for off-road racing – with less extreme wheels and tires it can run on the road. The rear engine gives good grip on rough going.

Ford sell these Broncos on the showroom floor in America. Tough pick-ups with big V8 engines are rugged and fast and can be modified to run at well over 100 mph on rough ground.

Ford Bronco

Street Freaks

Americans are generally (and rightly) proud of the fact that they can go one stage further than anyone else in just about anything you care to name. Certainly this is true of automobiles, where they can claim the biggest, quickest, most gadget laden, weirdest and most wonderful labels as their very own. America holds both wheel-driven and non wheel-driven land speed records, has the fastest, wildest dragsters, most powerful passenger cars etc.

derived from 'hot roadster' and it encompasses all manner of automotive lunacy. Hot-rodding began in the States in the 1920s and '30s primarily as a means of increasing performance, firstly for the street and then for the off-road, salt lake and desert speed trials.

In the 1950s off-road hot-rodding became more organized drag racing, and from this sprang a series of subsidiary cults, aiming primarily at performance. Alongside the speed merchants were the custom car fanatics who were devoted to individuality, coupled with extra performance, although not with competition as the main goal.

Lowest of the low – Los Angeles low-rider cult is wild. Bodies can be lowered right down to ground level with built-in jacks. Interiors and exteriors are generally beautifully reworked in amazing ways. This was once a '59 Chevy Impala.

Low-rider

Typical Model T hot-rod, immaculately prepared with fiber-glass replica bodywork and pick-up bed at the rear. Note the skinny dragster look at the front, fat rear wheels and tires to transfer that supercharged Chevrolet power to the road. Trick paintwork is a mixture of 'fogging' and 'imagineering.'

And in the world of off-beat street machines, they show the rest of the world the way.

A great many car cults began in America, in particular on the West Coast, in and around Los Angeles and San Francisco. Hot-rodding is a term

The big fad for hot-rods based on Model T, A and B Fords began in the 1950s and survives there today, and in other parts of the world too. Then there were fads for modifying current showroom cars, and cars like the Chevrolet Bel Air of 1955–57 vintage became classics in their own time as both custom and performance machines. There was a fashion for high-riding, a fashion for low-riding, both extremes of a movement which began in performance and then moved into the fantasy world of the customizer.

Model T hot-rod

Pony car

It didn't take long for the car manufacturers to realize that there was a whole new market available for the personalized performance machine, especially for the youth market, and during the 1960s came the pony car, the muscle car and the super car cults. Pony car was the name given to the new breed of sporty compacts like the Mustang, the Camaro and the Firebird which offered slick European styling in a compact, dramatic shape, coupled with a range of engine and transmission options which could give strong drag-strip performance right off the showroom floor. The quest for power also led to the muscle and super cars which were more or less performance engine and custom trick options on basic intermediate size American saloons — the Pontiac GTO and Plymouth 'Cuda are probably the best known.

The wildest hot-rods must be the Model T-based cars. While these can be built using genuine period chassis and body-shell from the 1920s, most T-rods use specially built chassis and fiber-glass bodies which can be most readily adapted to suit the needs of the hot-rodder — whichever engine, transmission, suspension he wants to use. Needless to say, very little on a T-rod is actually Model T except for the body, perhaps the overall stance and some

real life details such as lights, screen etc. There is a whole industry in the United States producing parts of all kinds for replica Model Ts so that owners can build up cars from scratch.

Whatever the cult, though, there is always a group who will take it to extremes, usually just for pure effect. The Los Angeles low-rider cult is one of the strangest — the idea is to make the car look and ride as low as possible, a theme which is generally carried out on the largest, grossest cars in America's styling history. In fact the whole low-rider cult can seem in bad taste — the cars are hideous, the customizing really kitsch, the interiors in appallingly bad taste, but all so beautifully executed and so pointless that it is fascinating.

Look and look again. At first glance it's a Chevrolet Z/28 Camaro, one of the hottest 'pony cars.' At second glance it's shrunk in the wash. In fact it is an ultra-short Volkswagen chassis carrying a miniature Z/28 plastic body.

One of the saner bodies to be produced for the VW, Brubaker Box looks smart and is actually practical with stylish seating for four on an L-shaped sofa in the rear. One door only — it slides for all occupants to gain access.

Brubaker Box

Ford 'Summerhouse'

A sort of summerhouse on wheels – this hot-rod oddity is built on a Ford 1928 pick-up with lift-on lift-off chalet back for camping.

Ford-based hot-rod

This 1934 Ford-based hot-rod retains original bodywork, 'channelled' over the chassis to lower lines and emphasize the power look of big rear wheels and exposed engine. This one is a fuel-injected, late model V8 for demon power.

The extreme in low-riding is to have the body actually touching the ground. This isn't for general road use, except for a few freaks who race on the street with the bodywork touching the ground in a shower of sparks. Most low-riders have a built-in jacking system which enables the body to be lowered or raised on the chassis. Cruise down to the drive-in burger, park and lower the jacks until the body sits right on the deck!

The high-rider cult is almost as pointless, although it did have its origins in drag racing, where the body was jacked up in order to transfer weight to the rear wheels on acceleration in order to improve traction. High-riders have amazing spacers to lift the body 9 to 12 inches above the wheels, exposing all the modified suspension and the fancy wheels. But these machines tend to be even less manageable on the road than low-riders!

Customizing is a fairly modern term in the car world. The Americans invented customizing, which means simply personalizing, and although adding individuality isn't a new idea, the modern extremes of customizing are essentially a post-Second World War phenomenon. At one time, all cars could be said to be customized since they were individually built, often to the purchaser's own design. Then as motoring became more and more part of people's lives, mass production turned out millions of cars all looking the same. And so more and more people wanted to make their machines different from the next – to customize, in fact.

The art of customizing takes many forms, from the addition of accessories to a production car, to drastic reworking of a standard machine, right up to building a car from scratch. After the Americans, the UK car owners are the most adventurous in their customizing, and some British machines could hold their own at any American custom car show.

One of the oddest UK customs was built for a millionaire playboy, Michael Pearson, who wanted not only a really individual custom car but also something that could stand up to the hurly burly of London traffic. So he acquired a Second World War Daimler Dingo scout car, as used in 1940, on the assumption that if it was bullet-proof, it must also be London taxi-proof. Originally the Dingo came with a cab, and to turn it into an open car involved hacking away two tons of armor plating. Away too went the old olive green drab finish to be replaced by a startling purple metalflake paint. Spartan interior had to go too — it now has smart bucket seats, wood and leather trim with stereo radio and tape player built in. When originally converted, the Daimler 6-cylinder engine and four-wheel drive was retained, but in the quest for thrust a powerful new American V8 Chrsyler engine was substituted.

A certain Mr John Bird also had individual ideas about a custom car — as long as it looked different, he didn't mind too much what it was or what other people thought about it. He started with an old 'granny' Rover 90, began hacking and snipping and ended up with a machine that attracts looks — admiring or otherwise — wherever it goes. The alloy bodywork was built solely by the owner and is all immaculately polished and finished. The most distinctive feature is the exhaust system, a snake pit of polished flexible piping and motorcycle exhaust pipes which occupies one side of the car. Now John Bird has a new project — a customized Bentley!

Even the most humble machines can make interesting custom cars and it's often the case that the wildest machine

Dragster style Model T hot-rod

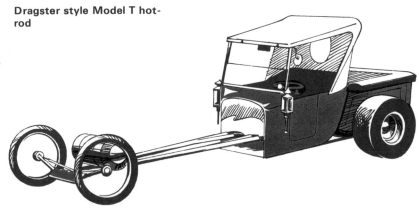

began with the most ordinary original — the Ford Model T, for example, the original mass production car, is the symbol of the American hot-rod. In the 1930s, in Britain, Morris was turning out thousands of cheap, dull Morris 8s. In the 1970s a young enthusiast took a touring version of the old 8 and turned it into a highly individual and well finished custom car which went on to win many show prizes. Most of the original bodywork was retained, along with the chassis. The bonnet was abandoned, though, exposing the engine which was by then a modified BMC Sprite engine, all highly chromed, painted and polished. The old radiator looked a bit ridiculous, so this too went, replaced by a specially made up rad looking a bit like a Rolls Royce shell. Fiber-glass wings, wide alloy wheels and tires, old brass lamps, new custom upholstery and metalflake

Austin 7 Chummy — hot-rod style

Taking the dragster front-end look to extremes. Believe it or not, this Model T-based hot-rod is actually legally in use on the road in California. Don't ask about the handling. Engine is somewhere at the back.

Lovable Austin 7 Chummy is now a cherished collector's item in the UK. No such reverence in America — this one's been turned into a compact street-going hot-rod with tough V8 power. Performance in such a lightweight chassis is beyond belief!

This bullet-proof custom town car was built on a Second World War Dingo scout car. It now features a powerful American V8 engine, custom paint and interior.

Customized scout car

Dad wouldn't recognise it – a 1950s upright Ford Popular which now has an American V8 engine, Jaguar independent rear suspension and a body that flips up in two pieces.

roads that's certainly no lemon — it is, in fact, an orange. This beautifully finished fiber-glass machine is built like a giant orange, complete with dimpled 'skin' and stalk. Underneath is a chassis containing a Mini engine and front suspension with twin rear wheels set close together. The interior is lined with matching orange deep-buttoned vinyl, with a driver's seat and two seats for passengers. The back segment of the orange hinges up for entry and exit.

Those are all strictly UK custom cars, but there is in Britain a group of enthusiasts who are devoted to American style hot-rodding and in particular to the Model T hot-rod. Hot-rods, or T-rods, are perhaps the wildest looking street machines with their replica Model T 'bucket' bodywork, completely exposed engine, skinny front wheels and huge rear wheels and tires which give the rods their odd nose-down stance. Nothing about a hot-rod has anything much to do with a vintage Model T, except for the overall idea and perhaps a genuine lamp, bracket or windscreen. The finest hot-rods use the Jaguar E type or Mk 10 independent rear axle and suspension which, apart from working very well, looks incredible when it has been fully chromed and polished and hung, exposed, at the back of a hot-rod.

Of more recent machines for a base for

paint finished off one of the best examples of a British custom car which not only looked good, but was also quick and manoeuvrable on the road.

In the custom car world, a machine that's badly done is generally known as a 'lemon.' But there's one oddity on the

Transformed Rover 90

a street freak, the sit-up-and-beg Ford Popular and the Morris Minor are two popular examples. The one shown is Pinball Wizard, named after the song from the Who's rock opera *Tommy*, and although it looks fairly standard at first glance, it is very different underneath. The body hinges up in two parts to expose the specially made chassis, which now carries a 335-hp Chrysler V8 engine and automatic transmission unit from a crashed Jensen Interceptor. Suspension is new, too, and at the rear is a Jaguar Mk 10 unit, hot-rod fashion, although not as highly chromed as most hot-rods. To support the front end and to provide good braking for the now very fast chassis, MGB suspension and braking were used.

Naturally anyone building a custom special like this doesn't follow any particular rules about what to use, and a clever customizer will make good use of whatever is available as long as it results in a safe, good handling machine. The front bonnet and wings hinge forward as one piece on this 'Pop' for access to the engine, and have been made in one piece in fiber-glass. It isn't necessary for the main bodywork to flip up, but the owner has entered the car in several custom car shows and likes to show off the chassis!

One important offshoot of the customizing community is the chopper bike and an offshoot, in turn, of the chopper is the chopper trike. This is really a combination of both car and bike, since it uses the front end of a motorcycle and the rear end of a car, usually a Volkswagen. Steering through a motorcycle front fork assembly, generally extended, chopper style, the fork assembly is then fitted to a lightweight frame carrying the

engine. The VW engine is generally used since it combines engine, gearbox transmission and suspension in one compact unit. Even the smallest 1200-cc VW engine gives an incredible power: weight ratio in such a light chassis, and handling is the biggest problem in a chopper trike since the front wheel, with little weight over it, tends to lift off the ground on acceleration. A motorcycle tank is usually used, sculpted and painted, and most builders use a high backed chopper seat, although trikes have been built with three seats abreast!

A stiff-upper-lip Rover 90 was the base for this wild looking street car, finished in highly polished alloy and chrome. Performance is good, too, with new lightweight body.

The answer's a lemon – or at least an orange. This Mini-based fiber-glass orange was built for fun and features lush interior seating for six.

Mini, Motorized orange

Grand Prix and GT Cars

Mercedes Grand Prix

Ahead of its time in build and performance, the Grand Prix Mercedes took first, second and third places in the French Grand Prix of 1914.

American Jimmy Murphy took the motor racing fraternity by surprise in 1921 when he beat the field to take the A.C.F. Grand Prix at Le Mans in his straight-eight Duesenburg. It was the first time an American had captured the title. During the race, Murphy set up a lap record of 83·2 mph — an achievement which was not to be surpassed until 1929.

Today, when we think of racing cars, we visualize sleek, low mechanical streaks of lightning that produce their very own brand of thunder. They are, without question, a breed apart. Industries have been built around them; multi-million dollar companies sponsor them; each year hundreds of thousands of dollars' prize money is won or lost by them; and adventurous young men risk their lives driving them.

But talk to the specialist about 'racing cars' and he'll ask you to be more specific, for since 1966 all competition cars have been defined in groups. There are series production touring cars, grand touring (GT) cars, sports cars, special touring cars, prototype sports cars, two-seater racing cars (i.e. sports-racing cars), cars defined under any of

the racing formulae (1, 2 and 3) and *formule libre* racing cars.

Today the motor racing calendar is chock-a-block with all sorts of competition events, each with its own detailed lists of conditions and stipulations — sometimes trying limitations, but ones which, in an age of such sophisticated equipment, are essential if only in the simple interests of fairness.

Many years ago, of course, it was a different story. In the very beginning there was little difference, apart from the attitude of the driver, between a car that was being driven for pleasure and one that was being raced. There were no 'specials,' 'sports' or other modified versions. However, such machines were inevitable — and as early as 1894 competition motoring had its beginnings in the Paris-Rouen Reliability Trial. As the title suggests, the race was more a test of reliability than anything else; the criterion was not so much how fast can she go, but how far! A year later the first real motor race took place, again on the roads of France (mainly because that was the only country in Europe with suitable roads; Britain at the time refused to allow racing on its public roads). This marathon, which took in 732 miles from Paris to Bordeaux, was won by Emile Levassor at the not-too-frightening speed of 15 mph.

Yet within less than 20 years, speeds were up by almost 100 mph on that figure. In 1914 the Mercedes company scored a staggering success in the French Grand Prix with their little 4½-litre racers, taking the first three places. These neat, white-painted cars were capable of an astonishing 112 mph.

Duesenburg straight-eight

One thing that hadn't been paid an awful lot of attention in these early years was the car's bodywork. So it was quite a shock for the Europeans when, in 1921, the American Duesenburg team arrived for the A.C.F. Grand Prix at Le Mans with a road-racing modification of an Indianapolis Duesenburg. The big 3-litre was a slick-looking piece of machinery, of sophisticated design and superbly finished. It finished superbly in the race, too: it came first, having covered 321·78 miles at an average speed of 78·1 mph.

As the years slipped by, and more and more manufacturers appeared, so the number of racing cars grew.

They came, mainly for reasons of prestige and publicity, from the same stables as the family motor cars. Good performances on the track could mean higher sales in the showroom!

As the motor industry began to grow up, and manufacturers found it more and more easy to sell their vehicles without the added expense of prestigious motor races, so many of the big names withdrew from competition motoring and left the business of squealing tires and hair-raising scrapes to the wealthy individuals and companies who wanted racing cars to be their only preoccupation.

Consequently, although some of the big names like Alfa Romeo and Mercedes maintained their interest in the

Porsche 917

but handsome in a fascinatingly aggressive sort of way, these are the creations of today's speed kings. In cold fact they are nothing but an engine on wheels with one seat cramped inside a long, low body, and an intricate system of shock-absorbers and springs. The track cars have no silencers, no horn, no mudguards and no lights.

Weird? Oh yes. But to the avid motor racing enthusiast, they are mechanical poetry in motion.

The dashing Porsche 917, which strolled to victory in the 1971 Monza 1000 kms at an average speed of 146·21 mph. Driver Rodriguez thrilled the huge crowds with his defiant, high speed display as he repeatedly broke the lap record.

The legendary John Player Special – officially known as Team Lotus 72D. In this strikingly attractive racer – it's finished in black and gold – Emerson Fittipaldi became the 1972 World Champion after winning the Italian Grand Prix.

John Player Special

sport, new names sprung up and, by the 1950s, a new breed of racing car was on the scene. Names like Cunningham, Lancia, Cooper, BRM, Vanwall, Maserati and Ferrari became the big attractions.

From the rounded, chubby shapes of these machines have developed the super-streamlined racing and GT cars that burn their way around the world's circuits, cars like the John Player Special Lotus and Porsche 917 pictured here. By no means beautiful,

Alfa Romeo

The 1940s and '50s saw many drastic changes in the basic shape and styling of racing cars. Typical of the 'new look' was this Alfa Romeo. The art of streamlining was beginning to be developed.

Car Trends

A trend that may have got out of hand: the expensive *Spirit of America – Sonic II*, the giant speed machine which Craig Breedlove dreamed up for the Land Speed Record run.

Built by the American Machine Foundry Corporation, this experimental safety vehicle (far right) is one of several prototypes constructed for developing the new 'safety' trend.

There's no shortage of offerings for the streamline trend. This beauty is a Lancia Fulvia 1·6 HF 'Stratos.'

Lancia Fulvia 1·6 HF 'Stratos'

Stand a Karl Benz three-wheeler of 1885 next to a modern piece of auto engineering like the Lancia Fulvia 'Stratos' and you have to admit that motor car trends have changed somewhat in the last 90 years. However, it's no secret that the luscious Lancia is not exactly the everyday family saloon, and this is the type of machine which is the main concern of the 'trend men' – the back-room designers who have to look into the future and try to work out what the next generation of motorists will be driving.

There are all sorts of considerations to be made: what will tomorrow's car look like?; by what will it be powered?; how fast will it go?; what sort of brakes will it need?; and, perhaps most important of all, how can we make sure it will be safe?

In America this last question has led to the building of an experimental safety vehicle. The government commissioned the project, and their brief was simple: produce a car that will 'escape damage in collisions at up to 10 mph with a solid object and in which no one would be killed in a 50 mph solid-object crash, a 30 mph side swipe or a 70 mph roll-over.' A tough order, but one which produced a very 'safe' piece of machinery, including energy-absorbing hydraulic bumpers, an anti-skid device, a protective roll-over cage, a periscopic view mirror, and air bags which inflate on impact from beneath the dashboard to prevent the occupants from being thrown against the windshield.

When it comes to setting the trends in record-breaking machines, though, safety is almost an incidental consideration. When Gary Gabelich took the Land Speed Record at a colossal 630·388 mph back in 1970 in the National Gas Corporation's *Blue Flame*, previous holder Craig Breedlove decided it was time for a new trend in *his* particular field of motoring. His proposal was *Spirit of America – Sonic II*, a three-wheeled, needle-nosed monster that would produce a mammoth 35,000 lb thrust.

But while Breedlove and company are thinking about the best way to burn fuel fast, the rest of the motor industry is working out how not to burn fuel at all. The oil shortage, along with the problem of pollution from exhaust emissions, means that the trend men are having to look at other means of power for the cars of the future. Whether it will mean reverting to steam or developing the electric car is to be seen. One thing is certain: the days of the internal combustion engine are numbered.

American Machine Foundry Corp's safety vehicle

INDEX TO ILLUSTRATIONS